THE PENINSULA

The Peninsula

A STORY OF THE OLYMPIC COUNTRY

IN WORDS AND PHOTOGRAPHS

BY Don Moser

SIERRA CLUB ◆ SAN FRANCISCO

The Sierra Club, founded in 1892 by John Muir, has devoted itself to the study and protection of national scenic resources, particularly those of mountain regions. All Sierra Club publications are part of the nonprofit effort the club carries on as a public trust. The club is affiliated with the International Union for Conservation, the Natural Resources Council of America, and the Federation of Western Outdoor Clubs. There are chapters in California, the Pacific Northwest, the Great Basin, the Great Lakes region, and the Atlantic seaboard. Participation is invited in the program to enjoy and preserve wilderness, wildlife, forests, and streams. Address: Mills Tower, San Francisco; 25W45, New York.

PUBLICATIONS COMMITTEE
AUGUST FRUGÉ, *Chairman,* GEORGE MARSHALL, *Vice Chairman*
DAVID BROWER, *Executive Director,* BRUCE M. KILGORE, *Secretary*
ANSEL ADAMS, FRANCIS P. FARQUHAR, MARTIN LITTON, ROBERT C. MILLER,
WALLACE STEGNER, EDGAR WAYBURN (*ex officio, president of the club*)
Manufactured in the United States of America by Chas. R. Wood and Associates
Designed by David Brower

*For My Mother and Father
In gratitude for their putting up with
salamanders and cricket frogs, and
in gratitude for a few other things
besides*

FOREWORD

This is a book about a young man's love affair with a peninsula.

Every one of these subtle and exact photographs and every line of the text is a step in the search for communion with an essence, an essence that is loved the more, the more it is known and understood.

This book is like a holding of hands, like a looking into eyes. A quiet book and a gentle one, it is also absolutely clear-eyed, and the fact that it is clear-eyed never reduces for an instant its respect, even awe, in the presence of natural things. The Olympic Peninsula, it means to say, is not merely a topography and an ecology, a natural and delicate balance among all the interacting life forces, plant and animal, bacteria and mold, moss and tree and man. It is a miracle as well, and worthy of wonder.

These photographs and their accompanying text do not so much tell a story as record a deepening of comprehension and feeling. The approach is a poet's: Mr. Moser delights in sensuous things, the visible, the touchable. Whether he turns his camera upon a starfish stranded on a dawn-struck beach or upon the austere snowy peak that John Meares in 1778 named Olympus because it seemed a fit home for the gods, he gives his concentrated still attention to what he is examining. Because from his Ohio boyhood onward he has been a biologist and an outdoorsman, he sees with the eye of knowledge, precisely, without romantic fuzz; and though this is a book warm with feeling, the feeling is held in, down under, showing only between the lines.

It is the precision of this book that makes it special. Every object—shore rocks, tide-washed kelp, islands looming in mist, sun on mountain water, a sea-worm cluster, a moss-grown log, a mountain trail in druidical shade—is searched for what makes it passionately itself; and every object, so viewed, contributes to a growing sense of the wonder of natural things.

Even man, normally a destroyer to be feared worse than fire. Mr. Moser understands as well as the next the dangers that man represents. But these weathered faces and figures in worn jeans that he shows us have made their peace with the peninsula, submitted to it. Indian or white, they have become as native as the Olympic elk or the Sitka spruce or the salal brush. They have adapted themselves to the peninsula's natural pace; their cutting edges have been blunted, their muscles relaxed, their clatter quieted, their eyes cleared. Living in and with and by the natural environment, they have become part of it: models in a simple way, as Mr. Moser is in a more complex one, of a harmony between nature and man.

Since the years when he worked as a summer ranger in Olympic National Park, Don Moser has been a writing fellow at Stanford University, a Fulbright scholar and editor in Australia, a *Life* reporter, and finally an assistant to Secretary of the Interior Stewart L. Udall. I believe that he has not re-visited the Olympic Peninsula since he left it six or seven years ago. But I think I can still see the peninsula in him, as I see it in his book.

The kind of love that shows through these photographs and between the lines of this low-keyed, casual, often humorous text is not the kind of thing a man loses. It is in him like a newly-grown organ, as vital a part of him as the air-bladder is of a fish. He balances by it, rises by it when he chooses.

It is not true that you can't take it with you. On the contrary, once you have achieved it, they can't take it away from you.

The Peninsula is one of the splendid books about the mystical and strengthening bond between nature and the man who will submit himself. Short of submitting to the Olympic Peninsula itself, I can think of no finer way to get this healing communion than by submitting to the words and pictures that record Mr. Moser's love affair.

WALLACE STEGNER

Greensboro, Vermont
July 17, 1962

THE PENINSULA

THE SEA

Here is the Peninsula.

Of course there's a lot more to it. The Olympic Peninsula in Washington runs maybe a hundred miles from Tacoma at the bottom to Cape Flattery sticking out into the ocean at the top. The center is filled with mountains, all blue rock and glacier ice, and long river valleys choked with some of the biggest, thickest timber in the world.

A lot of the Peninsula—almost a million acres of it—is in Olympic National Park, which means that the country is so special that it will be preserved pretty much as it is, from now on. Every year thousands of people come to visit the park—some to climb the mountains, some to make pack trips into the forest, some to go clamming or smelting on the ocean beaches, and some just to look.

Outside the park, although this isn't what you'd call a populated piece of country, there are a few towns—Port Angeles; Forks, where the big fire was; Sequim; and, believe it or not, Pysht, Lapush, and Humptulips.

There are some tourist lodges, some canneries, and some mills.

Occasionally on the Peninsula there's a little disagreement between the park people and the mill people—the tree people and the timber people is another way of putting it—over whether a particular piece of land should be turned into park or turned into lumber. But for the most part everyone gets along.

Living here there are people like my district ranger Elroy and Boli the Indian, one old man who collects stones and another who collects junk, and people like Gordon. Most of them have been around here for a long time, and they all live close to the country. In fact, sometimes it's pretty hard to tell where the country leaves off and the people begin.

I came out that summer from Ohio to work as a seasonal ranger for the park, and was assigned to Kalaloch District, the strip right along the ocean. I lived in a little cabin that was half buried in salal brush, with a woodstove to cook on and a half-grown raccoon for company. From the front steps of my cabin a man with a good arm could have pitched a rock clear over the salmonberry and knotty cedars on the bluffs and into the high tide. The roar of the surf was something I went to bed with at night and got up with in the morning; it was a little like living in the same room with an ocean.

I soon learned that wherever you are here, you are always aware that you are on a peninsula, that there's salt water all around you — the Hood Canal, the Straits of Juan de Fuca, or the sea. When you're in the mountains you can see the ocean, and in the forests you can feel it in the fog that drifts over the salal brush and up the valleys. And always, no matter where you are, you can smell it.

And before I'd lived here very long, I learned something else—that everyone around here looks to the sea for something.

Little Indian kids from the ramshackle village at Queets roam the beaches after storms, hunting in the driftwood for blue glass balls—the floats from nets of Japanese fishermen—that have been swept half way around the world by the currents of the Pacific. The kids sell the floats by the basket along the coast road, and what they have to sell is worth more than anything they get.

It seems that everything you could name winds up sooner or later on that treasure heap or junkpile of the seashore. The sea brings worn timbers from shipwrecks on the Pacific and hulks of rotting whales. It brings pale balloons of men-of-war and great turnip-shaped holdfasts from the ocean plants, strange fish, and clots of kelp.

And the sea brings driftwood.

All summer the driftwood lies around against the bluffs; women pick up chunks they like to carry back to Seattle and Tacoma, and the Indian kids tilt and balance along the logs that are piled house high and interlaced like jackstraws. When the storms come they pick up the driftwood and carry it away. But they always bring more from somewhere else, so that down on the beach you find a pair of great stumps sitting solidly on the sand, looking as if they had been there forever.

All the animals of the coastland live off the sea—the otters that play down in Kalaloch Creek in the evening, and the little bandit-faced raccoon who lives in the cedar swamps behind my cabin, and the bears. Down on the beaches I find their tracks, and a scatter of bones, an empty shell, on the waved sand.

The gulls live off the sea.

The Indians make their living from the sea. All afternoon the brown women sit down on the beaches waiting for the smelt to run. Sometimes they come every day for a week and sit all day watching the gulls and waiting for the smelt, and then at the flood tide they climb back up the steep trail to the bluffs, with their fine nets dry and their buckets empty. Then one day the coasting gulls drop into the half tide and someone sees silver flicker in the breaking water. Up and down the beach all the women jump to their feet, run out knee-deep into the surf and dip their nets into each bursting wave, and bring them up hanging with little silver fish.

The men like to get into their old dugout canoes with Johnson outboard motors on the back and go roaring up and down the river, or plough out the river mouth past Hoh Head into the big breakers. But when the kings are running, the big salmon coming up from the sea, the men go fishing too.

Very early one morning, at the lowest minus tide, we went clamming. Ace, the campground caretaker, and my boss Elroy and I took gunny sacks and the short-handled narrow spades called clam guns, and we went prowling up and down the beach in the fog and half dark. After Elroy had shown me what to do I walked along the sand, watching carefully for the small round pits that were the clams' blowholes. When I saw one I dug down as fast as I could, and of course the clam started digging too. It was a race between me and the clam, with the clam always winning. Soon my fingers were scratched and bleeding from groping in the sand; I was wet all over from a big wave that had run in and caught me as I knelt over a hole, and I was shivering with cold. But finally I reached into a hole up to my arm-pit, and feeling around in the wet sand my fingers touched something hard and sharp. I brought the clam up and looked at him, fat and yellow.

"How you doing?" came a voice over the sea roar.

"Swell," I said. "I got one."

"Good," said the voice, and Elroy went past in the fog with a big gunny sack full of clams over his shoulder.

And so I sat down on a rock and watched the fog burn away and the morning begin.

Sometimes you find things you're not really looking for. One morning at low tide I walked down to the shore. At first I saw nothing but the morning sea, and long rolls of sand-smoothed rock.

But then I looked closer.

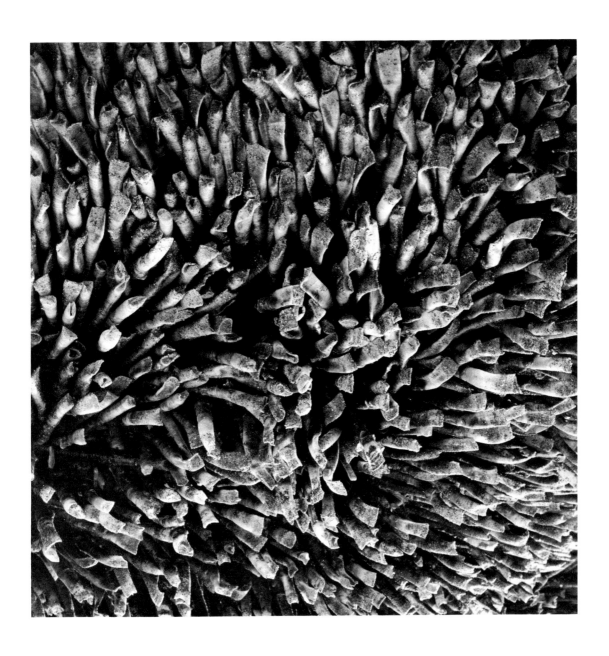

The rocks were clustered with glittering barnacles and rock oysters and bunches of tubeworms that would fill a bushel basket. There were fronds of kelp, their air bladders floating them on the small pools that lay in rocks; anemones that pulled themselves into shapeless blobs when I touched them; starfish, blue and orange and covered on top with bright tubercles. They lay handlike on the sand.

There was so much life.

Everyone talks about going to Destruction Island someday. From Kalaloch beach you can see it squatting darkly, right on the horizon. We all know that it is just a little patch of dirt covered shoulder-high with salmonberry and salal, that there is nothing there but an old house and a low tower with the light we see at night and the deep horn we hear coming through the morning fog.

But everyone talks about going there. Ace has always wanted to, and Elroy, and Boli the Indian. Even the Old Man mentioned it once, and he's lived here close to forever.

Perhaps it's because of the name. Or perhaps because, lying way out on the horizon, it seems as if it might contain all the things we can never quite get our hands on.

Or maybe the island is only an excuse. Maybe the place where they all really want to go is the sea itself—they'd just like to go on out and see what's there.

THE PEOPLE

ELROY was my boss on Kalaloch District. He'd been a park ranger for quite a few years, and he had a way with number nine wire. He kept a big coil of it in the fire cache, and whenever anything had to be made or fixed, that's what Elroy went after.

And he could use a rope. We had a chunk of one-inch hawser for rescue work. I was glad we never had to rescue anyone with it, because I could hardly lift it off the peg: But Elroy could make it do anything he wanted, and when he coiled a picket rope he would stand there not even looking and throw it into perfect looping figure-eights over his hand.

What Elroy liked to do was get out in the country and prowl around, or take his coil of wire and go fix something. The Park Service has its administrators, just as any other organization does, and most of them are men like Elroy. You might wonder what a man like that does when he has to come in out of the country and sit behind a desk in some park headquarters.

Well, I can tell you one thing he does. He looks out the window.

One of the first people I got to know on the Peninsula was Ace, the campground caretaker. I'll never forget his stalking through the garbage dump up to his knees in garbage, picking up beer bottles with one hand and with the other squirting the swarming flies from a can of insect spray, and muttering over and over again, "That'll put the quietus on them, by God!"

Ace was a husky little man of about sixty-five. Before he became caretaker he'd been a logger, a railroader, a fisherman, and a junkman, and he'd put the quietus on dogs, horses, flies, ornery burros, and men, all across the Northwest. But now he was a little deaf and a little forgetful, so that sometimes he'd drive his old International pickup for two or three miles in second gear until I would remind him to shift into high.

He lived in a tent in the campground with a mean, feisty little terrier, a lot of odds and ends of junk he'd collected, and a big stack of *Alaska Sportsman* magazines that he read at night by a Coleman lantern.

He'd never quite outgrown his junkman days, and he always went through all the trash and garbage from the campground, looking for things that were valuable only to him: old Ford gaskets, hunks of wire rope, beer bottles, a good stick of two-by-four. From time to time he'd go into the second-hand stores in town and swap some of his junk for some of someone else's. In that way he thought of himself as a kind of businessman.

But if you ask me, Ace just had the collecting urge.

Ace had always dreamed of buying his own fishing boat and going to Alaska to live out his days. He'd been saving and swapping junk for years, trying to get money enough together, but something always came between Ace and his boat.

Sometimes when we stood on the bluffs overlooking the sea he would spot a fishing boat so far out I couldn't see it at all. "Out there, boy, on the *hor*izon," he would say, accenting the first syllable.

Finally I would see it, a white speck on the blue water. "I'm gonna get me one of them yet," Ace would say. "I'm gonna outfit her up and take off for the Aleutians and the salmon grounds, go to Ketchikan and Juneau and Anchorage and all them places I read about. I had some bad luck so far, but by God, I'm not too old to do her yet."

Hugh was a big hairy man with a bit of poetry about him. One evening we were standing on a bridge over the Quinault River when a gull came slipping up from the sea, high and clean in the sun. We watched it as it went over, whipping up-river in the wind, then still watching it Hugh said quietly, "I wish I could fly like that."

I was sitting by the picture window in the lodge at Kalaloch one night, watching the sunset and the otters playing down in the neck of the creek. At the bar there were two Indians who'd been drinking steadily for some time. It was easy to tell how long they'd been at it, for each had been keeping score by pinning the little plastic mixing sticks through the front of his shirt, and by now both looked as if they had bandoliers strapped across their chests.

A group of guests came into the bar, and one of them said, nodding toward the Indians, "I didn't know they were allowed in here. Liquor is supposed to make them mean." He meant to speak softly, but the words carried in the small room.

One of the Indians got up from the bar. Tall and lean and gray-haired, he stood there swaying and looking at the guests. Then without a word he walked on out, the other Indian after him.

Later, as I was walking back to my cabin, the same Indians picked me up in their rattly old Buick. The tall Indian told me his name was Boli. I said that I was the seasonal ranger on the ocean strip, and when I explained that I worked with Elroy, Boli grinned at me over the back of the seat. "You come on home with us for a while," he said. "We'll have some beers and talk."

When we got to the reservation the old house that he lived in was full of Indians. Boli introduced me around to them and to his wife, a small bright-eyed woman who watched him anxiously. The oldest of the four or five kids, a boy of about fifteen, leaned against the wall and looked at me with a straight face. And there was a little boy of five or six I'd seen playing dirty faced along the river. He had large brown eyes and dark hair. Sitting down on a chair, Boli picked up the boy with one big hand and set him on his lap.

"This here is my pal," he said.

There were a few oleographs on the wall of the room, and a beautifully carved model of a war canoe, some clothes drying next to an oil heater, a big Rayonier calendar, fishing poles leaning in a corner, and a Johnson five-horse outboard clamped over the back of a chair. "We don't live so good," Boli said. "We live pretty primitive, you might say." He fondled the boy in his lap. After a moment he said, "Me, I'm in the Lions' Club. Only Indian in the Lions' Club. You think anybody else in the Lions' Club lives like this?"

Boli bent over the child, who remained impassive, sucking at a thumb. "We fix um, huh, kimosabe?" he asked the boy. "Us Injuns go on warpath, scalpum paleface, uh? Get um up, Scout!"

Boli started to laugh, but then he stopped to look around the room fiercely. The others, embarrassed, I suppose, by seeing him talk this way before an outsider, said nothing.

"My own fault," Boli said softly. "I can make ninety, hundred bucks a week when the kings are running good." He flexed one of his big arms. "Make it in the woods, too, if I want to. Everytime I get the money I think I'll do something about this place, fix it up. But then I get the money and it's in my pocket, and I want a new motor"—he waved at the Johnson clamped over the back of the chair—"or a shotgun or some damn thing, or something for the kids. And I figure, hell, I got a house—it's not much of a house, but we been living in it a long time and a while more don't make much difference."

Boli looked at the little boy in his lap. "It don't make a damn anyway," he said. "Our kids live good. They ain't too clean but none of them got T.B. You look at this whole village. All the kids live outdoors along the river and in the woods and on the beach. And not a one of them got the T.B."

The little Ohio town where I went to college was a town populated by old women. It seemed that every second house up and down the streets was owned by some old woman, all alone, who rented out rooms to college students. I used to wonder where all the old men had got to.

Then I came out here, and I found out. They're all rattling up and down the Northwest in beat-up pickup trucks, doing jobs of work with their hands, and living in cabins or tent houses or logging camps or cheap hotel rooms. Wherever they live, it's generally neat as a pin, with one black suitcase in the corner, one pair of highly-polished, finely-cracked black shoes under the bed, and a pile of magazines, precisely stacked, on a chair.

The old men can cook better than you'd think, and they always wash their dishes. They read more than you'd think, and you'd be surprised if you knew all the thinking they did, and what about. They've got the time for it.

Old John was a carpenter, maintenance man, shake-cutter and Jack-of-all-trades. He was a man of about sixty who looked and talked as if he had been hacked from a cedar burl, and he liked coffee that looked like ink and poured like molasses. I'd come in and John would be standing over the old iron woodstove, balancing a cup of coffee against his paunch with one hand and stirring some stew with the other.

"Have a cup of coffee, son."

I would decline.

"Well," he would always say, "that's your privilege, son. That's about all a man gets out of life. What he wants to eat and when, and a few kicks in the tail. That's about all there is to her."

One day I was out by the woodpile with Don. He was chopping stove lengths, and I was sitting on a stump fooling with one of his six-guns. Don reached out for it. "This here," he said, "is the road-agent's spin." The gun flashed and revolved in his hand. "Nothing to her," he said.

I tried it myself. *Thump* went the gun on the ground.

"It takes a while," Don said. He went on talking while he chopped and I practiced. "Now there's fanners," he said, "and there's thumb-busters. Me, I'm a fanner, but Keith was a thumb-buster. Remember that Blackhawk?" I remembered seeing the gun he spoke of back in the cabin—it had been stripped. "Cheese and crackers," Don said. "Soon as Keith got that gun he filed off the sights, trigger and trigger guard so she'd draw smooth. First time he shot it, she wound up ten foot away in a snow drift.

"That's Keith's way, though. When we lived together, Keith would never allow no electric lights. Said folks get too dependent on them modern conveniences. Wouldn't sleep in a bed. Said, 'You never heard of no Indian sleeping in a bed, did you?' But that's just Keith's way."

Don didn't stop chopping as he talked. He stood a slab of wood on the block, and with smooth fast strokes of his double-bitted axe he split his stove lengths off. The slab never teetered on the block, never moved, and chunks of wood fell off one by one as if they fell from a machine.

"Thing about Keith was, he didn't just talk it, he lived it. Now that's one way, but then there's another way. Take Julian. You know what happened to Julian last week?"

"No," I said.

"Shot hisself."

"He did?' I said.

"Yup. Practicing his fast draw, and shot hisself right in the cheeks." Don slapped his rump. "Yessir, right in the cheeks. Doc never took the bullet out of him, neither. He's just going to be sitting on it, from now on."

On Sundays there was heavy visitation on the ocean strip, and it was best just to be around. So I'd wear a full uniform and tie, even up the dents in my Stetson, and cruise the beach road, talking to the visitors and helping anyone who needed it. Around ten thirty I'd stop at the lodge for a cup of coffee, and often I'd run into Bert, the state fire warden, a chunky, grizzled man in his mid-fifties.

Bert would be wearing his battered tin hard hat and sitting on a stool at the counter, hunched over a cup of coffee. He'd look at me out of his little blue eyes, crack about the federal boys never having to work, and shift a ham of a forearm so I could sit down.

"Seeing any of the country, Don?" he asked me one day.

I told him that I'd spent the weekend on Hurricane Ridge, and that it had been beautiful up there.

Bert shrugged his big shoulders. "It ain't much any more," he said. "Not since they built that road. I used to go up in that country way back years ago. No roads then, not even trails most places — it was way before CCC. I'd beat the brush up the Elwha into high country, and stay up there in the meadows — flowers all around. Then you could stay up there all summer and not see a soul. Game — big herds of elk — you could hear them bugle on the ridges. That was nice country then — best I ever seen.

"It's not the same now. They built trail so anybody could get up who could walk a couple dozen miles. They then built road so anybody who wasn't afraid to drive it could get up. Now the new road's finished, there'll be people all over the place.

"I don't go up any more. I don't want to see it. But I suppose the mountains are still all right. Not much they can do about the mountains."

I was up-river at the old Smith ranch when Gordon, the park packer, rode out of the timber leading his string of mules and scrub horses. He'd brought a load of cedar shakes to use in fixing up the old ranch house. Helping him to unpack his string, I began taking one of the alforjas off a pack saddle.

"Hey!" Gordon said: "You stay away from that old Jordan mule 'n outfit. You give that ornery bastud a chance and he'll kill you 'n outfit."

And so I went over and admired Gordon's saddle horse. She was smooth-muscled and golden and well knit, with fine light-tan leather and a plaited bridle Gordon had made himself. "That's a fine looking animal," I said professionally.

Gordon squatted, nodded. "Thaousand dollar quarter mare," he said. "Got papers on her. She's a little buzzy from the racetrack 'n outfit, but I'll work it out of her on trail this summer."

We went over and sat on the porch. "Got a tailormade?" Gordon asked. I gave him one. We lit up and talked about horses 'n outfit.

It was an odd feeling, reading so many books and seeing so many movies about cowboys, and now really knowing one—a real professional, and him just a lean tired man in torn Levis and a four-day stubble, just an ordinary flesh-and-blood man with no place to go in particular, sitting on the porch of an abandoned ranch and watching his pretty grazing mare through quiet eyes.

One day when I was working in the big timber along the Queets Road, a car pulled up and stopped, and a man got out. I could tell by the shine on his shoes that he was a visitor, and I could tell that he was mad.

"Ranger," he said, "what kind of a gyp-joint are you running here? I only get two weeks vacation a year. I've come out here two thousand miles to see something, and I've been driving around this place all day and all I've seen is trees."

But it takes all kinds.

A lot of people who visit the Peninsula are from big cities. Where they come from, if they want to look at a tree they have to go sit in the park. When they get out here, there's always a few like that man in the forest, but there's another kind as well. They don't say anything at all. They just look.

And I guess I know why that is.

I've seen the answer all around me.

THE FOREST

ELROY'S idea of teaching Bob and me about horses was to show us how to saddle the big ornery scrubs we had on the district, how to pack the alforjas and throw a diamond hitch, and then send us off on a four-day trip over the worst trail in the park—one that hadn't been traveled or opened in over a year.

"I'll look for you to be coming out down the Queets in four or five days," Elroy said. "But that's a real rough trail in there, and you're green, so if you can't get the horses through don't feel bad about turning back. Luck." And then he climbed into the stock truck and pulled away.

Bob and I squatted there finishing our cigarettes. We were both new seasonal rangers on the district, and neither of us had ridden a horse much since our childhood days on ponies at the county fair.

"I wonder what we do," Bob said, "if we hit a big washout or lots of down timber?"

"I don't know," I said. "I don't suppose it matters much if we don't go all the way through."

"I'd like to," Bob said. "My great-grandfather pioneered in a covered wagon from Indiana to east Washington. They must have had a lot worse than we're going to have."

We stayed there for a little, smoking and thinking about it, and looking at those horses. Then we mounted, Bob leading the pack horse, and we went into the forest.

[79

This is a forest of big trees—fir and spruce twelve and fourteen feet in diameter, and great cedars so thick their fluted trunks look like forests in themselves. Two hundred feet above, the plumes lock solid and block out the sun.

Windfall spines of trees criss-cross all around, so that off the trail a man would walk more on timber than on earth. Feathery young firs sprout from their roots in fallen logs, and in some places there are colonnades—straight lines of huge trees standing on stilt roots, the mother logs from which they grew long since rotted down to mold.

Sometimes on the trunks of the fir there are shelves of yellow bracket fungus, brilliant in all the soft greenness.

Every square inch of ground is covered with growth, layer upon layer of it. Every tree trunk, every fallen log, every branch, supports a whole community of life

For this is really a jungle. In this forest there is more rain than anywhere else in the country—a hundred and fifty inches of it a year.

And yet, in summer, the brush snaps like dry bones under the horses' hooves, and the stumps and bracken ferns are dusty along the trail.

This is a silent forest, though. Every once in a while you turn up a herd of Roosevelt elk, and the great half-ton bulls, their heads tilted back beneath the weight of their antlers, go prancing like show horses into the timber, and for a long time you can hear them whistling and crashing through the brush.

But most of the time when you stop along the trail, you will hear no singing insects, no birds, only the quiet.

You see trees in this country which you have to look at a couple of times before you can believe them. In the cedar swamps behind my cabin there is a cedar tree twenty-one feet through. And up the Queets, a little way off the trail, there is a tree seventeen and a half feet thick and over two hundred feet tall. The bark is thick and dark and scored in deep furrows, flaring out over buttressed roots. It is the biggest fir tree in the world. I couldn't say how old it is—five hundreds years, a thousand maybe.

All of them, of course, don't get a chance to grow quite so big, or live quite so long. Sometimes you'll hear a screaming on the mountain, and find a couple of big men with hard hats and Black Bear jeans held up by broad suspenders horsing a chainsaw into a tree.

Yellow sawdust spins out of the cut and covers their boots and covers the ground. Slowly they move the saw on through, feeling the drive of it right down to their heels, and sweat stains spread out across their denim shirts. You look up at the plume two hundred feet above, at the feathery topmost branches. You think you see a quiver, but you aren't sure until it comes again, the very top of the tree shuddering slightly. The men slip the saw from the wood, and not hurrying and still carrying the saw they back away from the tree. Then one of them calls, not saying or shouting but singing it out, high and clear over the mountain, "Timbahhhh, downnnn the hillll!"

Way above there is a shudder again, and then it moves, oh so slowly, the top deliberately turning down, then faster, but it is coming . . .

A new one will grow in its place, of course. You can log this country, or burn it, but give it time and the country comes back. The country can be washed away or covered under ten feet of windfalls, but even that doesn't stop anything. Sooner or later the trees find a way.

But it takes a long time. You find burn scars and logging scars here that are many years old, with nothing on them but snags and stumps and that marvelous stuff called fireweed that always comes to cover up the ugliness with tall spikes of purple blossoms.

No, it takes quite a while to make trees like the ones that grow up the Queets. Longer, I guess, than most of us have to wait.

On that first trip that Bob and I made into the forest we had no trouble at the beginning. The trail was good, but very steep. My horse Fran moved along smartly, and she was comfortable riding uphill. It was a relaxed and easy time.

On both sides the timber was thick, mostly fir with a little hemlock and cedar mixed in. I could look over my left stirrup far down into the canyon, and sometimes I could see the river twisting at the bottom. Across the canyon there was a waterfall only a foot wide with sword ferns growing thick along the sides. It dropped clean for two hundred feet, disappearing in white spray far below.

It's funny, the feelings a man can get when he's got a horse under him and some wild country around him—especially if both horse and country are new to him, and not things he can take for granted. This was one of those moments—they are pretty rare—when the only difference between life and what you see in the movies is that here there wasn't any background music. As we went sidling up that steep trail I felt as if I were a little bit of everyone from Daniel Boone to Meriwether Lewis to Jim Bridger. I wore a Stetson for a while, and then a fur hat, and then a forage cap. I had a Colt .44 on my hip, a Green River knife in my belt, and an octagon-barreled Hawken across the pommel. I kept one eye cocked for Sioux, Crow, Blackfoot, grizzly bear, and the U. S. marshal.

Pretty soon we started down into the canyon, the horses moving strongly under us, down to the fast river slicing between rock walls wet and green with moss and ferns, and the water crashing beneath us frothy white and green as bottle-glass.

94]

That trip didn't stay easy for long. There were windfalls and washouts, and it turned out that the horses had minds of their own. And then it began to rain — a real no-nonsense Peninsula rain. We rode along soggily, our jackets soaking the water up. The horses steamed and squelched; their flanks were matted down with water, and they looked as miserable as we did. It seemed as if the country was getting its annual hundred and fifty inches all in one day. I wanted nothing more in this world than to be dry for a while, and to be able to light a cigarette. When I looked at Bob and saw the water streaming down his face, I knew that he felt the same.

But finally the downpour slacked off a little as we came around switchback high on a ridge, and we paused up there. For just a moment the weather opened up, and far away we could see the Pacific lying bright blue in the sun. Then the rain began to close in again. Nearby two stunted cedars were intensely green, and past them and miles and miles below I could faintly see the forest and the gray river twisting through the valley.

I think you can get madder at a horse than at anything else on this earth.

I got separated from Bob once on that trip, and went on with Fran until the trail disappeared in the new grass of the meadows. We began to circle, watching for a rock duck, but Fran liked downhilling, and I had to keep reining her around toward the ridge. Finally I got tired of fighting, and tying her there I hunted the trail on foot. After I'd found it we switchbacked up until we came to the top of a snow-patch that fell away for a couple of hundred feet, steep as a ski jump, to a line of hard-looking spruce at the bottom. There was a shale wall above us, and brush and timber grew close along the edge of the snow. Dismounting, I kicked at the snow with my boot, finding it hard and granulated.

When I started back along the trail to see if I could find a way to get the mare down through the timber, I hadn't gone twenty yards before she nickered. She had started across on her own, and now she was stuck in the middle of the snow.

I worked my way across above the snowpatch to get in front of her. She was only twenty feet away, but she might as well have been across the canyon. She was frightened, and I knew that I'd never be able to get the axe off the saddle to cut her a trail. This is where I lose a horse, I thought, and I felt sorry for having called her all those names back in the last meadows.

With nothing else I could do, I began to talk to her quietly, but she only stood there, her feet bunched under her. But then carefully she lifted one foot and moved it ahead, tamping it against the snow until she made a hollow for her hoof. I kept talking and glancing toward that row of spruce trees at the bottom.

One foot at a time she inched across. Once or twice her hoof slipped, and each time I thought she was gone, but she managed to regain her balance, and she kept coming.

Finally she touched her hoof on hard ground, and I reached out for the bridle.

When we got to the meadow below I loosened the cinch and took off her bridle so she could graze a little, and I lay down in the grass to relax.

"You stupid old scrub," I said aloud, and she looked up at me with her big soft eyes.

"Ah, go on," I said.

By the time we dropped down into Tshletshy Creek there wasn't much trail left. One of us went ahead to chop out logs and find the trail, and the other followed, leading the horses. We had to stop so often that there was no point in riding, and besides, the downhilling was making us a bit tender. Once in a while a log eight or ten feet thick would be lying slantwise across the trail, making a hopeless obstacle until we found out that the pack horse was pretty trail wise, and if we let him go he'd pick a way around through the windfalls that we could follow with the other horses.

But then we came around a switchback to a gully sided with shale and dirt dropping about seventy-five feet to the creek below. The trail that angled across the cut had been washed out, leaving nothing but a bare dirt wall.

"I guess that does it," I said.

We scouted back along the trail, but the windfalls were too high and the sides were too steep. There was no way to get around. We had nothing for digging, only the axe, and we needed that sharp for cutting windfalls. "We didn't bring a file, did we?" I asked.

"No. Maybe we could use one bit for this and keep the other sharp."

"It would still take forever to cut a trail across that with just an axe."

Feeling pretty dismal, we sat down and smoked a cigarette. "You know," Bob said finally, "I keep thinking about my great-grandfather. I mean I wonder what would have happened if he'd come to something like this and decided he couldn't get through."

"I guess he'd never have made it to Washington," I said.

"I guess not," Bob said.

And so we got out the axe and went to work. We had a big sheath knife, and we used that too. Since we couldn't stand on the steep bank, we cut out little hollows for our knees and knelt there, holding the axe right behind the head and chipping away.

It took a long, long time, and before we finished we were worn out and thirsty and soaked with sweat. But finally we had a little trail chipped out, and we moved the horses on down, and stopped for a drink of water.

On the last day of that trip we rode into the clearing of an abandoned ranch a few miles up-river from the ranger station. Both of us were tired, with four days' beard and dirt to the eyes.

"How do you feel?" I asked.

"Like a pioneer," Bob said, squinting across the clearing into the sun. "Look there." He pointed toward the little cabin. Elroy was there, waiting for us.

We rode up to him and dismounted.

"See you made it," said Elroy.

"Yeah," Bob said.

"Pretty rough?" Elroy asked.

"Nothing to it," Bob said. I looked at him standing there. His face didn't show a thing.

"That's what I figured," Elroy said.

THE SETTLERS

THERE is an old figure of speech about opening a door to the past. Around here it's not just a figure of speech.

All up and down the Peninsula you come upon the grown-up clearings in the forest, the crumbling houses filled with rotting, rusting odds and ends of people's lives, skeletons of hummingbirds in sinks and nests of mice. Maybe a barn, and inside a rusty plow—you can push your thumb right through the share—hangs from straps on rafters; jars of flaking bolts saved to fix something never broken, jars of preserves, black now, broken tools, and twisted chunks of oakum. Maybe an orchard, the trees with rusty crosscut saws wired around the trunks, teeth down, to keep the bears away, the branches mossy and thick with little bitter apples.

It seems as if you are always coming to the doors, and you can never keep from going in.

[105

They were just about the last pioneers who came up these river valleys. One of them was a big, black-haired Irish gambler named Martin Killea, who came brawling down from Alaska about the turn of the century. He found some good level land in the aspen bottoms up the river; he cleared the ground and made a homestead. He lived there and worked his place, and after a while he died.

All there is left now is a pile of rotten cedar shakes in the field behind the ranger station and a crooked sign bearing his name on a stream that dries up in summer. In a little while the shakes will all have been burned for kindling in the stove at the ranger station, and the crooked sign will fall down and never be replaced, for the stream isn't even on the maps.

One evening I crossed the river, and in a big meadow there I found a rail fence squaring off a little plot of ground, and inside the fence a tumble of ferns and blackberry vines, and four gray wooden slabs driven into the ground. On one of them, the letters so worn that I had to touch the wood with my fingers to read them: MARTIN KILLEA, AT REST.

Most of them have gone where Martin is, but some are left, like Harry. He'd lived there in the woods on the Pacific Coast for years, but he still sounded as if he'd just stepped outside Boston for a look around. Harry was a stocky little man with quick pudgy hands and a missing finger. Waving and gesturing, he talked so fast that I could hardly follow him, and then he would stop abruptly and stick his hands in his belt over his fat belly, rock back and forth on his heels and say, "Hmpf, Hmph," as if agreeing with himself.

Harry played at farming, but mostly he went down to the beach to look for stones and driftwood which he took back to a little house that was like a museum. There he smoothed and varnished the driftwood and polished the stones, and lived with them as if they were people. I said before that everyone around here looks to the sea for something; I guess Harry just looks to it for more than most.

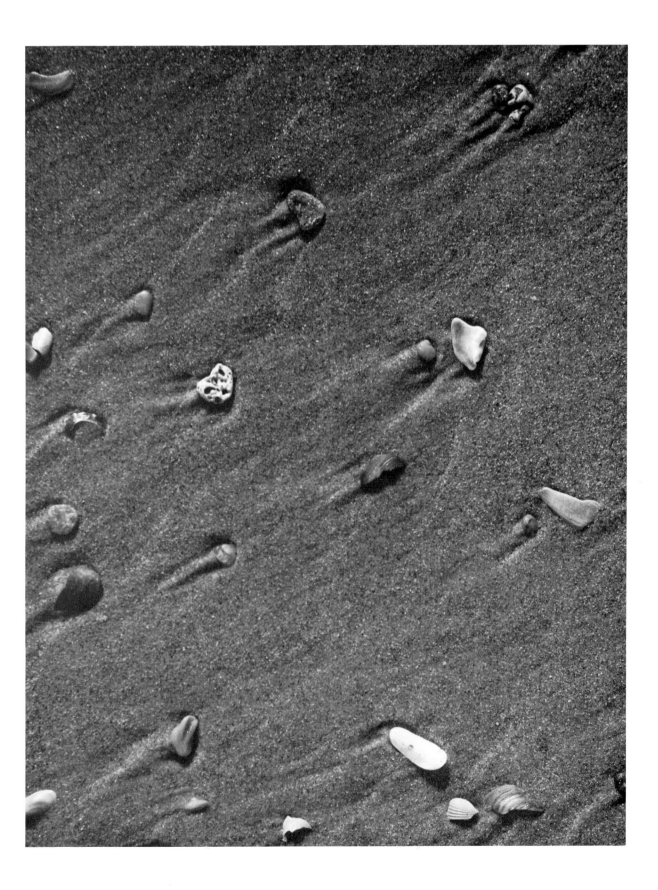

Not far from Harry's there was another clearing. The place was small and lost in the forest, and the house was weathered and gray, with boards coming loose along the walls. But behind the house he had built on the land he had cleared, old Andy grew flowers.

I stopped late one afternoon and found him working in his garden, down on his knees, humped over, with the moist soil on his hands and his thin gray hair stringing down his face. Together we walked around the flower beds, and he told me about them shyly, how those snap-dragons—those with petals like white fur—had won a grand prize the year before, and how well the glads were doing this summer, seeming as he said it like a little boy.

I looked at the soft brilliant flowers and then around the clearing at the forest of huge spruce and dark fir jammed solid with centuries of windfalls and moss and ferns, crossed by trails of elk and bear and cougar, and I thought, "You're crazy. You can't come here—a little fumbling old man—and scratch a hole in this wilderness and live in a brokendown cabin and grow those beautiful flowers."

"There they are now," he said, and pointed to the edge of the forest. The doe came out first, slowly, hesitantly, then the two fawns. Together they walked into the meadow, and as we stood watching them, began to graze.

And I suppose that was my answer.

The Old Man had lived on the bluffs overlooking the ocean since before there was a park or anything else. After he got old and the park came he built a few cabins so he could make enough to live on by renting them to the weekend tourists. But there was no plumbing, and the power plant kept breaking down, and he was so feeble he couldn't keep the place clean. Finally the authorities said he couldn't operate any more unless he fixed up his place. But he was too old to do it, and couldn't afford to hire anyone, and so he just left it that way and wrote letters back filled with pathetic misspellings and bitterness.

One day he came down to the station, his loose dirty clothes flapping around him, and asked me to help him fix his power plant—he'd taken it apart himself, then couldn't get it together again because his hands weren't steady enough to thread on the small nuts.

After we got there I had to shout to make him hear that I needed some tools—a crescent wrench and a screwdriver and pliers. When he finally understood he pawed around in the trash on the floor until he found them. But after I got the wiring connected the engine wouldn't start. The old man told me to switch the wires around. I didn't know much about power plants, but it was obvious that the wires were in the right place. I argued with him and wound up shouting to make him hear, but he just kept saying, "I think you ought to change the wires around."

And so I did, finally, to please him. It took half an hour, and as I worked at it I wondered how he could have lived with the power plant and depended on it for years, and still not know a thing about it. At last I got it together his way. Of course there wasn't even a spark, and he couldn't understand that.

I still don't know whether he was too old to understand the power plant, or if he just misunderstood out of contrariness, as if that damned twentieth-century gadget wasn't worth the trouble.

Most of them are gone, but you still find little pieces of them left.

One night Paul came into the bar at the lodge, where we all sat to watch the big sunset over Destruction Island and the otters playing in the creek, and he had with him a piece of driftwood hanging from a rusty chain. He got a hammer and a nail, and as he hung the chunk of wood on the wall he told us the story.

Once an old Dutchman came with his daughter to the Peninsula and built a cabin in the forest. The old man said that he didn't like people, and he lived as if he meant it. On the rare occasions when he went to town he spoke to no one, handing the shopkeepers little slips of paper on which he had written his needs. Near the edge of his property along the road there was a spring of cool fresh water, but the old man kept a shotgun loaded with rock salt to discourage those who would drink it, or for that matter, to discourage any other callers.

Then his daughter put together her few things and ran away to Seattle, and after that the old man lived alone. One day he went to the ocean and walked the beaches until he found a piece of smoothed and silvered driftwood. Then he forged a chain, pounding out the red-hot links on his anvil, and he carved a message on the piece of wood. Finally he hung the finished sign on a tree near the spring.

The sign had fallen down years ago, not long after the old man's death, but Paul, who prowled around a lot, had turned it up and brought it in to hang in the lodge.

All of us gathered around to see. In the dim after-sunset light we could barely make out the faint and weathered lettering:

If you go bey and thirsty be,
The fault's on you and not on me.

And one day in an abandoned house where ferns grew from the floor, there was a book, damp and yellow, a school book. And on the flyleaf, very faint now:

I guess you dont know how much you mean to me. You dont know how your treating me but maybe you know what your doing. Stella told you bunch of lies I guess and you fell for them like you did for her.

There was an abandoned ranch miles up-river from the end of the road, and one evening when Elroy and I were out on the trail we decided to spend the night there. It was in good condition still, with a woodstove and a fireplace, big wooden bunks, and rough, faded curtains on the windows.

After we watered the horses and ate supper we built a fire of old shakes in the fireplace. On the back of a shelf Elroy found a bottle of bourbon, left, I suppose, by some fisherman who'd used the place. There was enough in it for two good drinks. We mixed the whiskey with cold water from the spring, and sat in front of the fire sipping the drinks and leafing through some old *National Geographic* magazines.

In the corner was a bookcase. I looked at the titles on the shelf, seeing there all the stories of adventure that I'd read as a boy back in Ohio—Paul du Chaillu and Ernest Thompson Seton and Kipling's *Plain Tales from the Hills*, each with a faint scrawl on the flyleaf—from the sister to the brother on his birthday.

I thought about the boy who lived in the middle of this wilderness and read and reread those stories, and how lonely it must have been for him here, about how much the books must have meant, seeing him shyly accepting them from his sister on that day every year, then lying in the firelight and reading them over and over. And I felt a little sad about it until I thought of him walking onto the porch at evening to see elk grazing in the meadows, then in the dusk going down to the river to watch the trout rising and swirling from the deep water.

I took the Kipling over to the fire and lay down there in the brightness. I sipped the drink slowly, saving it, and read one of the stories—"Lispeth"—and remembered reading it so many years before, liking it then, and liking it now, perhaps even more now.

Elroy had found an old wind-up phonograph in the dark corner, and some warped records, and being Elroy he tried to make it work. Something was broken, and so he put the record on and spun the turntable by hand. But the record was so old and the needle so bad that I couldn't recognize the words or even the song—just a high, frantic voice with a harsh beat in the background.

Lying by the fire, I wondered what the boy had been like, and his sister and the man who built this house and laid the stones in this fireplace and made the clearing in the forest. I wondered how they had lived and how hard it had been and why they finally gave up and left, leaving so much of themselves behind, as though they'd just gone one day into the forest and never come back.

Sometimes you wonder how they did it with no more than they had—all of them who opened up the West—how they built what they built and crossed what they crossed and got through what they got through.

You wonder how they got out there in the first place. I've seen something of the mountains and the forests where there are no trails, and I know what that is. And I've crossed this country from north to south and east to west, and I would like to know how a simple man with only a wagon and a few oxen and a handful of crude tools could start off across that sweep of green and red and yellow land and expect ever, ever to make it.

But they did it. There were the men they built legends about, like Cougar Smith, and a man named John Huelsdonk, who somehow got a great iron cook-stove to his cabin miles up the Hoh River where there were no trails — people will tell you he carried it there on his back.

And the men that nobody ever heard of. In the forest you find the land they cleared and the trees they brought down, the stumps silver-gray with age and larger sometimes than the cabins they built from the timber.

Now what mark they made is slowly disappearing, as it's disappearing everywhere. The only difference is that this is a national park; other places what it's disappearing under is concrete, but here it's going back beneath the country.

And so if you think of them as having been in some kind of battle with the wilderness, then I guess you'd have to say that after the years they fought with the country and the folks they buried in it, all they ever did was lose.

But I think that what they did was win.

THE MOUNTAINS

WE stopped one day high on a spur in the cold wind. Sitting easy in the saddles, we looked out at the mountains standing away, ridge on ridge.

"It makes you feel pretty small, doesn't it?" he said.

"No," I said. "It makes me feel big. It makes me feel real damn big."

Everybody likes to get up in the mountains that fill the center of the Peninsula. Some drive their cars up the road to the Hurricane meadows; others ride horses along the ridge trails. And some like to do it the hard way.

There are a few who like to go right to the top. And some prefer that the hard way too. The harder the better.

It seems that people are always trying to find out why climbers climb mountains — that is, everyone but the climbers themselves. If you asked one, he probably couldn't figure out a rational answer if he tried; he would think it was a silly question.

My guess is that they climb for the same reason that in the year 1769 young Daniel Boone left the Yadkin Valley and moseyed across the Appalachians into Kentucky — and for the same reason that later on, when he was 65 years old, Daniel set out to stroll all the way to Missouri. Like Daniel, those climbers have an itch that nothing back in the cities is a salve for, and that people aren't a salve for either.

As a matter of fact, there's only one salve for that kind of itch. And I don't have to tell you what it is.

Although some don't show it as much as others, just about everyone I've ever met has that kind of itch, and I've got it too. And so one day I started out on horseback up the valley of the Quinault to spend some time in the high country. There is a place up there where you ride through broad grassy meadows, with the sheer cliffs of Muncaster Mountain on your left, shooting up clean for two thousand feet. All along the cliffs there are tiny waterfalls, some only six inches or a foot wide. They drop from the lip of the rock face in misty cascades all the way down to the river. All around there are big mountains, and the glint of snow patches and small glaciers.

The Peninsula is a place with good names on it—Three Prune, Happy Four, Whisky Bend, Staircase, Duckabush, and Dosewallips. I don't know who it was who named this valley, but it sure wasn't the same person who named the rest. This is called Enchanted Valley, which is too bad, because nobody likes to be told what they're supposed to feel. But I don't suppose it really matters what you call it.

Later on, up in the high meadows, I found a wooden post, an old trail marker of some kind. I stopped beside it to look at the country, and when I happened to glance down at my feet I saw the body of a fawn, long dead. There was no odor, no decay: Only the skin was left, soft and dappled with white spots. The fawn was unbelievably small and fragile looking, no longer than my forearm. A lion got it, I suppose, or maybe it just died there all by itself. A tiny thing like that, with legs like pencils in this wild land — I wondered how any of them could live at all.

But up in the mountains everything seems to live and grow in spite of common sense. Just look at the flowers and you know. Down in the river valleys where there's never any snow or cold, everything grows tall and thick, using all its living stuff to make great trunks and roots and branches. But up here, where the summer is gone under ten feet of snow before it's got fairly started, everything grows little and tough, and puts all its energy into a don't-give-a-damn rampage of flowers.

The flowers don't even wait for the snow to leave in summer. Little green spikes push up through the edges of the drifts, and a foot or so farther out the glacier lilies are in full bloom, making a narrow yellow ring of flowers that contours around the melting snow.

It doesn't matter where you go. Up on the wind-smashed rockpiles of the talus slopes, or through the alpine meadows, you look down at your feet, and there are the flowers.

You could say that things up here have vitality.

The country is hard, and a lot of creatures, like that fawn, never make it.

But there are always some that do.

On that first trip into the high country we got to the pass in the late afternoon. I left Fran in the meadows, and picked and climbed my way up onto a high ridge. It was a steep, long climb, and when I finally came out onto the crest I lay down there with the blood thumping in my ears.

And then I looked up.

Now where I come from back in Ohio there are no mountains. But when I was eleven or twelve, on those gray November days when you can smell the first snows coming, I would put on my warmest clothes and go out into the woods or around our place. There in that flat country I would stand perfectly still, moving only my toes inside my boots to keep them warm, and I would think about mountains. I had never seen any, but I'd seen pictures of them and read about them, and that smell of snow coming always made me think of them. I thought that someday I would live alone in a cabin in the mountains and go out every day on the rock and the cold glaciers.

But then I'd wake up to where I was, and I'd go home.

And so that day up on the ridge I lay there for a long time, and I felt in touch with things.

I mentioned vitality.

Out here you find it in the tidepool life down on the seashore. In the forest you find it in the young trees growing up from burn scars, fallen logs. You find it in the mountains.

The vitality is all around, and some of it rubs off on the people. On Ace and Elroy and Boli, on Harry and the old man who grows flowers up the river.

I wouldn't say that getting out in the country always makes a man happy. Life here is as full of disappointments as it is anywhere else—in fact, around here the disappointments are part of the scenery.

But what I'm trying to say is, the country has something to give, and Ace and Elroy and Boli and Harry have found out what it is. And every year thousands of people come out from Seattle and Tacoma and the big cities back east, and they find out too.

There aren't too many places like this left. Wherever you go in the West you can hear the clank and thunder of a big bulldozer working over the scenery or the snarl of a chainsaw up on a ridge, and on the highways you see the Mack and Auto-car and Kenworth log trucks come ramming past with black smoke spouting from the exhausts and whole stands of fir swaying in chains behind.

Now let me say that I think a Kenworth diesel is just about as beautiful a piece of machinery as has ever been made, and the men who drive them are, for the most part, men you'd have a hard time disliking.

There's only one thing I object to about those log trucks. They've got a big appetite.

Well, we've already decided to keep a lot of the Peninsula as a national park. This is one place where we've figured that we can get something more from the country than the money we might get from selling the trees.

What we have really decided, I guess, is where our roots are.

All I can say is that the country is a kind of great big powerhouse for something that vitality isn't quite the word for, but that's as close to it as I can get. And if we decide that that's the thing that really matters, the Peninsula will always be around — the coastland, the forest, the mountains kept pretty much the way they are, the way they've been. People from the cities can come out, and young kids who've never seen a big tree or a real mountain, and their kids will be able to come out too.

They can all come out and plug themselves in.